A prototype DB2, used for testing engine development, in front of the old airport hotel at Hanworth Air Park, Feltham, Middlesex, in 1950.

THE ASTON MARTIN

Alan Archer

Shire Publications Ltd

CONTENTS

The pedigree established: 1914-25 3
A reputation enhanced: 1926-40 7
Many more cars and successes:
1947-59 17
Touring in the grand manner:
1958-70 25
Even grander touring 29
Further reading 32
Places to visit 32

Copyright © 1989 by Alan Archer. First published 1989. Shire Album 228. ISBN 0 85263 980 5.
All rights reserved. No part of this publication may be reproduced or transmitted in any form or by any means, electronic or mechanical, including photocopy, recording, or any information storage and retrieval system, without permission in writing from the publishers, Shire Publications Ltd, Cromwell House, Church Street, Princes Risborough, Aylesbury, Bucks HP17 9AJ, UK.

Printed in Great Britain by C. I. Thomas & Sons (Haverfordwest) Ltd, Press Buildings, Merlins Bridge, Haverfordwest, Dyfed SA61 1XF.

British Library Cataloguing in Publication Data: Archer, Alan. The Aston Martin. 1. Aston Martin cars, to 1981. I. Title. 629. 2'222. ISBN 0-85263-980-5

Editorial consultant: Michael E. Ware, Curator of the National Motor Museum, Beaulieu.

ACKNOWLEDGEMENTS
The author is grateful to Neil Murray for sharing his unique knowledge of the earliest cars and to Jeffery and Stephen Archer for their forthright comments on a draft. Thanks are due to Aston Martin Lagonda Limited, the Aston Martin Owners Club, Louis Klemantaski, the Quadrant Picture Library and Roger Stowers for their great help with photographs from their collections. The cover photograph was taken in 1988 by Fred Stevens and other photographs are from the collection of the late Ted Inman Hunter.

Cover: *A DB4 made at Newport Pagnell, Buckinghamshire, in 1961.*

One of the production side-valve cars in 1924. This has a body by W. W. Hall.

'Coal Scuttle', the first Aston-Martin, at Highgate on 6th June 1919. The competition history of Aston-Martins started at 10.39 ½ pm, when 'Coal Scuttle' started the London-Edinburgh trial, driven by Jack Addis, the works foreman. It won a gold medal.

THE PEDIGREE ESTABLISHED: 1914-25

The incorporation of Bamford and Martin Limited in January 1913 formalised a partnership between Lionel Martin, a wealthy gentleman, and Robert Bamford, a gentleman engineer. Their small workshop in Henniker Place, London, soon became well known for tuning Singer Tens, on which Lionel Martin was a familiar sight at hill-climbs, trials and, in 1914, at Brooklands.

The intention to build an Aston-Martin was first reported in *The Light Car and Cyclecar* in October 1914. The curious coupling of the name Martin with Aston, taken from the Aston Hill climb in Buckinghamshire where Lionel Martin had competed on a Singer, secured a place near the top of alphabetical lists. While the first car was being built an Isotta Fraschini voiturette served as a test bed for its engine, commissioned from

Coventry Simplex Limited. The Aston-Martin was on the road by March 1915 and had covered 15,000 miles (24,000 km) by June 1919, when it won an auspicious gold medal for Jack Addis, the works foreman, in the Motor Cycling Club's London-Edinburgh Trial. It acquired the fanciful nickname 'Coal Scuttle'.

It was not until the end of 1920 that the second car, the production prototype, was finished in larger premises in Abingdon Road, London. It had a three-seater, 'clover-leaf' body and a 1389 cc side-valve engine. Lionel Martin, the dominant partner, won a gold medal in its first competition, the MCC Land's End Trial in March 1921, and its first race, at the Essex Motor Club's May meeting at Brooklands. The 1486 cc four-cylinder side-valve engine which was to be used in

3

Lionel Martin on the prototype at Brooklands on 7th May 1921. With the same 1389 cc engine as 'Coal Scuttle', it won its first race, the Essex Short Handicap.

production cars and the third car, 'Bunny', appeared in mid 1921. 'Bunny' lapped Brooklands at 83.28 mph (134 km/h) in August, finished sixth in the Grand Prix des Voiturettes at Le Mans in September (with a rabbit's tail mascot attached) and broke the Brooklands test hill record in February 1922. Kensington Moir, 'Sammy' Davis and Clive Gallop took ten unlimited world records a month later and the car was second in the Junior Car Club's Two Hundred Miles race against strong opposition in August.

In October 1921 *The Autocar* described the prototype as almost ideal for 'those gradual bends which have to be taken with great certainty and decision when driving at speed', adding that it attained 'more nearly to perfection than is the case where price has to be kept down'. Such can equally be said of all later Aston Martins.

Following disappointment with a 1487 cc sixteen-valve, single overhead-camshaft engine in 1921, Count Zborowski financed two cars for the French Grand Prix in 1922. These had sixteen-valve, twin overhead-camshaft cylinder heads based on Marcel Gremillon's design derived from Ernest Henry's pre-war Peugeot engine. The magnetos failed on both cars at Strasbourg, but Zborowski was second in the Grand Prix at Barcelona in 1922 and 1923.

Full-scale production did not start until 1923, with a choice of specification: either standard, with 8 foot 9 inch (2667 mm) wheelbase and 38 brake horsepower (bhp) engine; or sports, with 8 foot (2438 mm) wheelbase and 45 bhp engine. Most of the total of about 53 built from 1923 to 1925 had open bodywork by specialist carriage makers. Several were familiar sights at Brooklands.

A very narrow single-seater with a twin camshaft engine, 'Razor Blade', was built in 1923 to be the first 1.5 litre car to do more than 100 miles (160.9 km) in an hour. It lapped Brooklands at well over 100 mph, but not for one hour. Humphrey Cook's car, with a similar engine, crashed on the first lap of the 1925 Two Hundred Miles race, a sad result for Lionel Martin's last works entry.

Bamford and Martin had early been beset with the financial troubles to which

At Brooklands Track on Wednesday, May 24th, 1922

The **ASTON-MARTIN** *Car*

with side valve engine of 1,487 c.c., driven by Messrs. ⎰S. C. H. Davis
⎱H. Kensington Moir
⎱Captain R. C. Gallop

BROKE THE FOLLOWING

WORLD'S RECORDS

15 hours at 75·99 m.p.h.		1,100 miles	HRS 14	MINS. 30	SECS. 24·42 at 75·82 m.p.h.
16	„ 76·20 „	1,200 „	- 15	46	52·00 „ 76·04 „
17	„ 75·02 „	1,800 kms.	- 14	44	10·52 „ 122·14 k.p h.
18	„ 70·85 „	1,900 „	- 15	32	48·70 „ 122·21 „
19	„ 67·12 „	2,000 „	- 16	20	23·59 „ 122·40 „

(Subject to confirmation by the International Federation of Automobile Clubs.)

In addition to these the following Brooklands Light Car Class Records:

7 hours. 12 hours, at 75·84 m.p.h.	MILES.
8 „ 13 „	600, 700, 800, 900, 1,000, 1,100 and 1,200 at 76 04 m.p.h
9 „ 14 „	KILOMETRES.
10 „ 15 „	900, 1,000, 1,100, 1,200, 1,300, 1,400, 1,500, 1,600,
11 „ 16 „ at 76·20 m.p.h.	1,700, 1,800, 1,900 and 2,000 at 122·40 k.p h.

We wish to express our thanks to Messrs. Anglo-American Oil Co., Ltd. (Pratt's Spirit); The Houdaille
Hydraulic Suspension Co., Ltd.; The Marles Steering Co., Ltd.; Pirelli, Ltd. (Tyres ; The Robinhood
Engineering Works, Ltd. (K.L.G. Plugs); Scintilla, Ltd. (Magneto); C. C. Wakefield & Co., Ltd.
(Castrol Oil); and the Zenith Carburetter Co., Ltd., whose accessories contributed to our success.

BAMFORD & MARTIN, LIMITED, 53, ABINGDON ROAD, KENSINGTON, W.8.

'Bunny's ten world records at Brooklands on 24th May 1922.

5

so many famous manufacturers have succumbed. Robert Bamford left in 1921 and Kate Martin, Lionel's wife, replaced him as a director. An approach for help to the Bristol Aeroplane Company, among others, was unsuccessful, but the firm was rescued by Lady Charnwood in 1924. Her son, the Honourable John Benson, who was also registered as a shareholder, designed a promising new 1490 cc twin overhead-camshaft eight-valve engine, which was displayed at the London Motor Show at Olympia in 1925, the first at which the company had exhibited. Unfortunately the money ran out and a receiver was appointed on 11th November 1925. The reputation of the Aston Martin as a leading sports car had been firmly established, at considerable expense to Lionel Martin.

Count Zborowski with his mechanic in one of the two twin-camshaft sixteen-valve cars at Strasbourg for the French Grand Prix in 1922.

The same car, still being raced more than sixty years later. This is the Aston Martin Owners Club St John Horsfall Memorial Trophy race at Silverstone in 1985.

The International, which was shown, with a saloon and a polished chassis, at Olympia in 1929.

A REPUTATION ENHANCED: 1926-40

The assets of Bamford and Martin Limited (amounting to little more than goodwill) were acquired by Aston Martin Motors Limited, which was owned in equal parts by Lord Charnwood and Renwick and Bertelli Limited. D. A. C. ('Bert') Bertelli, although born in Italy, had spent all but five years in Britain. He had gained wide engineering experience with Graham-White, Enfield and Allday, and Woolf Barnato and had raced before the First World War. W. S. Renwick, also an engineer, had had a recent inheritance. They had built one car, the engine of which had a single overhead-camshaft cylinder head with unique valve gear patented in 1924.

The new company was established in October 1926 in part of the factory built for the Whitehead Aircraft Company in Victoria Road, Feltham, Middlesex. A tourer, a saloon and a mock-up of a Sports model were shown at Olympia a year later. For the 1929 Motor Show the Sports had matured into the International with a four-cylinder dry-sump 1495 cc engine embodying the Renwick and Bertelli patent, a separate gearbox, worm-drive axle, a rugged chassis and bodywork by Bertelli's brother Enrico ('Harry'), who had an adjacent workshop.

Racing continued to serve both to improve the breed and to expose the cars to potential customers. In 1928 Bertelli therefore reintroduced the custom of entering works or team cars in major events. Numbered LM 1 to LM 23 (but

Kenneth Peacock driving LM 5 at Le Mans, one of the three team cars entered by H. J. Aldington, of Frazer Nash, in 1931. It retired with broken valve springs after 21 hours.

'Sammy' Davis (left), the team manager, with LM 8 at Le Mans in 1932. It was driven by 'Bert' Bertelli and Pat Driscoll and finished second in class.

not LM 13), these had many successes in their class; outright wins would have been improbable in competition with cars with bigger engines. The first two retired from the 24 Hour Race at Le Mans in 1928, but LM 7 won its class in 1931. In the Junior Car Club's Twelve Hour Race at Brooklands, in 1929 LM 3 was third in class, in 1930 LM 4 was second and in 1931 LM 6

and LM 5 took the first and second places. LM 6 also won its class in the Tourist Trophy race in 1931. Such well known drivers as George Eyston, Clive Gallop, Dr Benjafield, Humphrey Cook and Leon Cushman had driven them, it is said, simply for the fun.

By 1929 the company was in serious financial difficulty again. Percy Kidner

A 'Le Mans' 2/4 seater at Feltham ready for the 1932 Motor Show.

Outside the factory at Feltham, 'Bert' Bertelli in LM 10, the car he drove at Le Mans in 1933 with 'Sammy' Davis. They finished second in class.

9

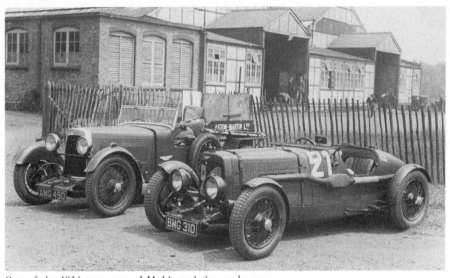

One of the 1934 team cars, LM 14, and the works van.

(whose Vauxhall company had been bought by General Motors) and S. C. Whitehouse replaced Lord Charnwood and John Benson in another new company, Aston Martin Limited. Renwick had left by March 1931 and R. Straker and N. Holder, of the distributors Kensington Moir and Straker Limited, had become directors. It was then the turn of H. J. Aldington, whose company, AFN Limited, made the Frazer Nash, to help. In exchange for providing a bank guarantee, his company became the main distributor and Aston-Martins were sold alongside, but at twice the price of, Frazer Nashes. This curious arrangement was short-lived and later in 1931 Lance Prideaux-Brune injected more capital. Stability was not ensured until the end of 1932 when Sir Arthur Sutherland assumed full financial responsibility and he and his son, R. Gordon Sutherland, joined Bertelli as the only other directors. Prideaux-Brune continued to exert a benign influence as the main London distributor at the Winter Garden Garage.

Substantial modifications were incorporated in the 1932 works cars, with the gearbox in unit with the engine, a bevel rather than worm-drive back axle and a lower radiator. LM 10 was first in

class at Le Mans and LM 8 was second, also winning the Rudge-Whitworth Biennial Cup. In 1933 LM 9 and LM 10 also finished first and second in class. The same modifications appeared on the 'Le Mans' model which was launched at Olympia in October 1932. Including its saloon and other variants, more than one hundred of this model had been built by the end of 1933, compared with less than 150 in the preceding six years.

Production of the last of Bertelli's 1.5 litre models started in January 1934. The Mark II had a strengthened chassis, a modified engine and many detailed refinements. Like earlier models, it was made as a short-chassis two- or four-seater, a long-chassis four-seater and a long-chassis saloon. A long-chassis drop-head coupé was available to special order. Three team car versions built for Le Mans had drilled chassis and lightweight bodies, but for trivial reasons LM 11, LM 12 and LM 14 failed to finish the race. In desperation Bertelli had the cars taken to the Isle of Man for the Tourist Trophy race painted bright Italian red rather than the traditional green. For whatever reason, LM 16, LM 15 and LM 17 finished third, sixth and seventh in the race, first, second and third in class and

10

The works team, including 'old' LM 7, and their support on the road to Le Mans in 1933.

A stop to refresh the drivers rather than to refuel the cars on the way to Le Mans in 1934? The early Mark II behind the works van was later owned by Sir Ralph Richardson, the actor.

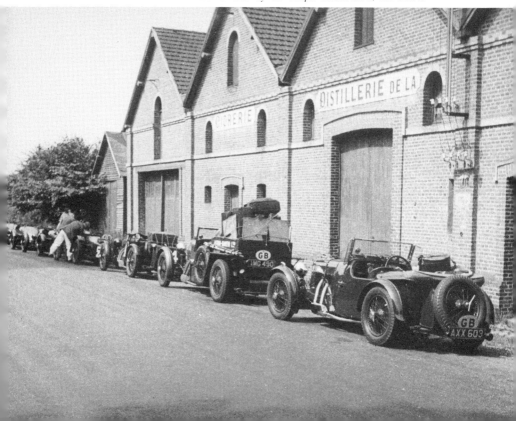

The prototype Mark II which served as the demonstration and experimental car, seen here in Glasgow at the start of the 1934 Royal Scottish Automobile Club's Scottish rally.

won the team prize.

The ultimate development of the 1.5 litre Aston-Martin, the Ulster, was on sale at the 1934 London Motor Show. This was a tuned two-seater short-chassis Mark II derived from the 1934 team cars and like them built with the particular care needed for cars intended for racing. The engine that had produced a modest 56 bhp at 4250 rpm in 1929 had been developed to give 80 bhp at 5250 rpm (and 85 bhp in the 1935 team cars). Few would disagree with Bertelli's view that this was his finest car unless great importance is attached to staying dry in the rain. Four works-supported Ulsters accompanied three new team cars to the 1935 race at Le Mans. This major effort was well rewarded as LM 20 was third overall (beaten only by a 4.5 litre Lagonda and a 2.3 litre supercharged Alfa-Romeo), first in class and winner of the Rudge Cup. LM 19 crashed, but three of the Ulsters were fourth, fifth and sixth in class, LM 18 was seventh and the other Ulster was eighth. This was a satisfying result on

what was to be the last appearance of a works team at Le Mans until 1949. Joined by LM 21, the works won the team prize in the Tourist Trophy race in 1935.

Although more Mark IIs were sold than any previous model, at prices ranging from £610 to £700, in 1935 sales were dwindling in the face of stiff price competition in the small sports-car market. To ensure survival, it was decided that the emphasis should shift to touring cars and saloons. The 15/98 (or 2 litre) tourer and saloon were launched in 1936 with a revised chassis incorporating hydraulic shock absorbers on the back axle and a 1950 cc engine based on the 1.5 litre. With the inlet and exhaust ports reversed, the larger engine gave 98 bhp at 5000 rpm. Although it had been well received at the Motor Show, the 15/98 was set back by prolonged teething problems and the price had to be reduced by £100 in 1938. A Speed model with a dry-sump version of the engine and, for the first time, hydraulic brakes was also introduced in 1936: some had two-seater

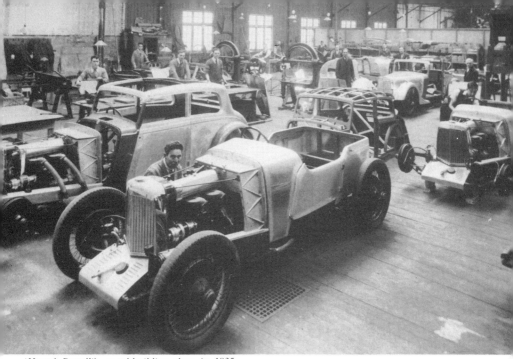

'Harry' Bertelli's coachbuilding shop in 1935.

Chassis assembly, 1935. The chassis frames were made by Rubery Owen Limited. A Mark II saloon and an Ulster are in the service area.

(Left to right) Charles Brackenbury, 'Bert' Bertelli and Tommy Clarke with LM 20, a 1935 team car. Jim Smith and Joe Bestane work on a production Ulster at Feltham.

Many cars were raced successfully by their owners. With LM 18 and two 'Le Mans', Donald Campbell, 'Mort' Morris-Goodall (who founded the Aston Martin Owners Club in 1935) and Dick Anthony won the Light Car Club's relay race at Brooklands in 1936.

'Jock' St John Horsfall in his 2 litre Speed model at Donington in 1938.

A Type C Speed model, among the last cars made before the Second World War, at Brooklands in 1939.

Ulster-type bodies. Two team cars, LM 22 and LM 23, were built, but not raced, by the works, but LM 23 had successes when driven by Robert Hichens and 'Mort' Morris-Goodall, as did Speed models in private hands, notably 'Jock' St John Horsfall's.

Bertelli left early in 1937, but Claude Hill, who had come with Renwick and Bertelli Limited from Birmingham, stayed to work with Gordon Sutherland on new models. Only the Type C, a Speed model with a steel-framed, streamlined body displayed at the 1938 Motor Show, had appeared before the Second

World War ended work on cars.

There was one very important exception. Hill had already tried many new ideas on a 15/98 dubbed, for no obvious reason, 'Donald Duck', but the 'Atom', not completed until mid 1940, was a major advance. Its chassis was formed from rectangular steel tubes and it had trailing-link independent front suspension. As predicted by Laurence Pomeroy in 1942, its performance provided a glimpse of 'the new order of motoring'.

From 1915 to 1940 fewer than seven hundred cars had been made, but at least half of them have survived.

The 'Atom' in 1942. This experimental car, completed in 1940, was a radical departure from earlier Aston Martins.

The first David Brown Aston Martin at Spa in 1948. It won this, its first and only race, driven by Horsfall and Leslie Johnson. Horsfall had helped Claude Hill with the development of this car from 'Atom'.

The first Two Litre Sports, in 1948. Later it was dubbed the DB1.

MANY MORE CARS AND SUCCESSES: 1947-59

The 'Atom' saloon, like 'Coal Scuttle', covered many wartime miles, latterly with its 15/98 engine replaced by a push-rod overhead-valve 1970 cc four-cylinder engine designed by Claude Hill. Unfortunately insufficient capital was available to develop the new car and the company was offered for sale, anonymously, in the personal column of *The Times* late in 1946. It was bought for £20,500 in February 1947 by David Brown. A few months later he also bought the Lagonda company, which in April 1945 had first tested a six-cylinder 2580 cc twin overhead-camshaft engine designed during the Second World War under the direction of W. O. Bentley.

By early 1948 a development of the 'Atom' chassis, with his push-rod engine but no body, was being tested on the road by Claude Hill, assisted by St John Horsfall. A new car was built for the 24 Hour Race at Spa in Belgium in only nine weeks, finished just in time for the final practice in July. Horsfall and Johnson drove this first post-war Aston Martin in

its first race to gain an epic victory for the new owner. The 'Two Litre Sports', later to become known as the DB1, appeared at the London Motor Show in 1948, but while the total of only fifteen was being built the marriage of the Aston Martin chassis and the Lagonda engine produced the DB2. Sutherland and Hill resigned in 1949. Frank Ayto, from Lagonda, became chief designer and was joined by Harold Beach in 1950.

Three prototype DB2s (only one with the 2.6 litre Lagonda engine) did not have great success at Le Mans in 1949, but the two entered at Spa two weeks later finished third and fifth. Horsfall, who had left in 1948, drove his much-modified 1936 Speed model single-handed for 24 hours to finish fourth. The DB2 was announced in April 1950 with a standard engine producing just over 100 bhp, or with a tuned Vantage version with a higher compression ratio and larger SU carburettors for which 125 bhp was claimed. It owed its road-holding and handling, precise and well mannered in

17

The modified Speed model in which Horsfall drove for 24 hours at Spa in 1949, finishing fourth overall, ahead of one of the works DB2s.

The works team at Le Mans in 1950, a 1949 prototype (middle) having been pressed into service after the third new car crashed on the way from Feltham. The drivers (left to right) are Reg Parnell, Charles Brackenbury, John Gordon, Eric Thompson and George Abecassis; the mechanics are Jack Sopp and Fred Lown. The sixth driver, Lance Macklin, must have been otherwise engaged.

The DB2 driven by 'Mort' Morris-Goodall and Nigel Mann on the Tour de France in 1951 and 1952, finishing fourth and second in class. They also drove this car at Le Mans.

the fashion of Lionel Martin's and 'Bert' Bertelli's cars, to Claude Hill's chassis. This had coil springs all round, trailing-link and torsion-bar front suspension, parallel linkages and a Panhard rod at the back. The chassis, engine and gearbox were made at David Brown's factories in Yorkshire and the cars with their elegant bodies designed by Frank Feeley were built in the middle of Hanworth Air Park, only half a mile from the pre-war factory in Victoria Road, Feltham.

The 1950 team cars did well at Silverstone and in the Tourist Trophy race and gained first and second in class and the coveted first place on Index of Performance at Le Mans. However, it was becoming apparent that international races would be won only by specially designed cars. Eberan Eberhorst, who had developed the pre-war Auto Union racers, was therefore recruited and John Wyer joined to become manager of the racing team. By September 1951 the two lightweight DB2s and one of the older cars which had done very well at Le Mans and in the Mille Miglia had been joined by the

first DB3. This had a new large-diameter tube chassis, a de Dion back axle, inboard rear brakes, a very light body and the 2.6 litre Vantage engine until prototype 2922 cc engines were available in 1952. Four team DB3s were raced with mixed success in 1952 and in 1953 until its replacement, the DB3S, was ready. Six more DB3s were sold and raced by their owners.

The lines of Feeley's DB3S body have remained much admired and its appearance was matched by its performance on the tracks. Between 1952 and 1955 the output of the 2.9 litre engine with Weber carburettors was increased from 147 to 240 bhp by use, for example, of a twin-plug cylinder head. Disc brakes were fitted to the front in 1954 and to all four corners in 1955, while wishbone front suspension and petrol injection were used on a team car in 1957. In 1953 the works cars won all their races, except the first, in the hands of such regular drivers as Reg Parnell, Peter Collins, Eric Thompson and Roy Salvadori, but 1954 was an almost unmitigated disaster. Suc-

19

About a quarter of the DB2s were drophead coupés.

Works DB3s, with 2.9 litre engines, being shipped to the United States in February 1953 for the Twelve Hour Grand Prix of Endurance at Sebring. Parnell and Abecassis were beaten only by a 5.4 litre Cunningham and the car driven by Peter Collins and Geoffrey Duke crashed when leading. The third was a practice car.

cess returned in 1955 when Collins and Paul Frère were second at Le Mans and first in class, a result repeated by Stirling Moss and Collins in 1956. In addition to ten team cars, twenty DB3Ss, including three fixed-head coupés, were sold for private use.

After more than three hundred two-seater saloons and about one hundred drophead coupés had been built, a pro-longed dispute in the body shop at Feltham resulted in Mulliner winning the contract to build the bodies for the first revision of the DB2, the DB2/4, launched at the 1953 London Motor Show. The rear window was enlarged and hinged to open, and by moving the spare wheel and the petrol tank and changing the roof it became just possible to seat two passen-gers in the back. The 2.6 litre Vantage engine was fitted until the 2.9 litre was in production in 1954. The acquisition of the Tickford company in Newport Pagnell, Buckinghamshire, at the end of 1954 restored an in-house body-building capacity, which led to the introduction of the DB2/4 Mark II, with such differences as a slightly higher roof and a less cumbersome bonnet, at the 1955 show.

Above: *1954 was not a good year for the racing team. Frank Feeley (right) looks at the remains of two DB3Ss and a Lagonda at Feltham after Le Mans, where two other DB3Ss retired.*

Below: *Stirling Moss driving a works DB3S with characteristic precision at Goodwood in 1956. Frank Feeley's bodies, of which this is the second of three DB3S styles, remain much admired.*

The body of the DB2/4 Mark II was built in the Tickford Works at Newport Pagnell, Buckinghamshire. The cars were assembled at Meltham, Yorkshire.

A DB Mark III driven very successfully by George Constantine for Elisha Walker (right) in the United States in 1957 and 1958; the small air intake is non-standard. This car returned to England to start a new racing career in 1982.

An attractive fixed-head coupé was added to the range. Assembly of the cars was moved from Feltham to Meltham, near Huddersfield, West Yorkshire. By March 1957, when the DB Mark III, the final development of this series, was announced, the Tickford works had been reorganised to enable everything except the gearboxes to be made under one roof. The 2.9 litre engine had been re-designed for the Mark III by Tadek Marek and was offered in four stages of tune. The compound curves of the front of the DB3S were incorporated in the bonnet and have remained a feature of later models. Automatic transmission as an extra, for which very few opted, and front disc brakes on a production model were other innovations.

Ted Cutting started to design another

This DBR1 driven by Roy Salvadori and Carroll Shelby brought victory at Le Mans in 1959, 31 years after Aston Martin's first entry.

The only DBR3, in front of the two DBR2s, at Silverstone in 1958 for its only race. It retired when its 3 litre version of the DB4 engine failed. The DBR3 was converted to become the DBR1 that was second at Le Mans in 1959, driven by Louis Trintignant and Paul Frère.

sports car, the DBR1, in 1955. Its small-tube space frame, gearbox combined with the back axle and twin-plug engine were all new. When first raced, in 1956, the capacity was 2493 cc but this was increased in 1957 to 2992 cc by lengthening the stroke, when it gave 240 bhp. Although the bore, stroke and power were the same as the DB3S engine in its final form, with a light-alloy block it was lighter and there was scope for development. In 1955 Marek had also started work on a 3670 cc engine for the replacement of the Mark III. In 1957 a racing version was fitted in the DBR2, which used the backbone chassis built for the unsuccessful V12 Lagondas. By 1959, with a twin-plug head and the capacity increased to 4164 cc, this engine was giving 315 bhp.

The four team DBR1s and two DBR2s greatly enhanced the Aston Martin's reputation. Although they could be driven legally on public roads (unlike many so-called sports cars) they collected eleven first, ten second and two third places from 1957 to 1959. With Tony Brooks, Jack Fairman, Jack Brabham, Stuart Lewis-Evans, Carroll Shelby and Louis Trintignant added to the list of drivers, there were three wins in the 1000 Kilometre Race at the Nurburgring. In 1959 the Aston Martin became the first British car to prove its superiority by winning the World Sports Car Championship, following victory, at last, at Le Mans.

There had been more than one abortive start on another grand prix car. The grand prix regulations for 1958, the availability of a suitable 2.5 litre engine and the successful DBR1 chassis, which could easily be modified, enabled the ambition to be fulfilled by building the DBR4. The first was tested at the end of 1957, but concentration on the sports cars caused its first race to be postponed until May 1959, at Silverstone. To the delight of some and the surprise of more, Salvadori equalled the lap record and finished second behind Brabham's rear-engined Cooper. Despite many modifications, a new cylinder head, fuel injection and different suspensions on two new cars (the DBR5s) in 1960, it was clear that these front-engined cars had arrived too late on the grand prix scene. The best that they could do was to finish sixth (driven by Roy Salvadori) in both the British and the Portuguese Grand Prix in 1959.

The worldwide reputation of Aston Martin was reflected in the high proportion of David Brown's first 1800 cars that was exported.

Roy Salvadori driving a DBR4 in the Italian Grand Prix in 1959, from which he had to retire with engine trouble. His car was some 230 pounds (105 kg), 16 per cent, heavier than the winning rear-engined Cooper.

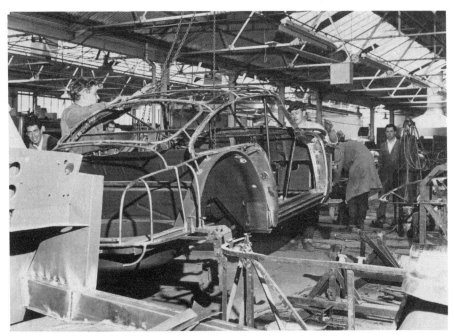

The body of a DB4 being built using Touring's Superleggera system.

TOURING IN THE GRAND MANNER: 1958-70

Much had changed in the world of motoring between the time when the DB2 was conceived and the mid 1950s. The successor to the Mark III, its direct descendant, would need to take account of the growth of the idea of the grand touring car in which great distances might be covered safely and in comfort at high cruising speeds.

The DB4, on which work had started in 1956, was completely different to the Mark III with which it shared the stand at the 1958 Motor Show. Harold Beach's chassis was a very strong steel platform with wishbone, coil spring and anti-roll bar front suspension. The live rear axle was located with parallel trailing links and Watts linkage. All four wheels had disc brakes. Touring of Milan designed the body, built by their Superleggera system with the aluminium panels fixed to a tubular steel frame. Four people

could be carried provided that not more than two had long legs. Marek's six-cylinder, light-alloy 3670 cc engine, first used in the DBR2, had twin overhead camshafts and two SU carburettors (three for the Vantage version available in 1961, when a convertible was also announced). The ability to accelerate to 100 mph (160 km/h) and stop within thirty seconds exemplified the DB4's remarkable performance. For those wishing to reach 100 mph six seconds earlier and content with only two seats, the DB4GT was revealed at the 1959 Motor Show. With a wheelbase 5 inches (130 mm) shorter, lighter-alloy body panels and Borrani wheels, 185 pounds (85 kg) had been saved. Three twin-choke Weber carburettors, a twin-plug head and higher compression ratio increased the power from the 240 bhp quoted for the standard engine by 62 bhp. As the much larger fuel tank left far

25

Grand touring elegance: a 1961 DB4.

One of the nineteen DB4GTs with a body built in Italy by Zagato in 1960 to 1963. Some would say these are the most elegant of all Aston Martins.

One of the two DP 214s being tested at Silverstone.

The prototype DB5 had somewhat unorthodox modifications for the James Bond film 'Goldfinger', with Sean Connery, in 1964.

less room for luggage, the GT suffix was not so much an abbreviation of grand touring as a forerunner of the regrettable 'go-faster' interpretation of the mass-producers. Nineteen of the 95 DB4GT chassis had extremely elegant, even lighter bodies built by Zagato in Milan.

In 1959 the prototype DB4GT won its first race, at Silverstone, but retired at Le Mans. The works returned to Le Mans in 1962 with DP 212, based on the DB4GT but with a de Dion back axle and a 3995 cc engine, a piston of which failed. The two DP 214s entered in 1963 were only nominally based on the DB4GT. They had special bodies similar to DP 212s, but with lightweight box-section chassis frames. The third 1963 team car was DP 215, which ran as a prototype with a dry-sump 3995 cc engine and experimental front and rear suspension. The DP 214s were the first cars to exceed 300 km/h (186 mph) on the Mulsanne straight and DP 215 reached 319.6 km/h (nearly 200 mph), but all failed to finish the race. Happily the David Brown racing era ended with successes when Salvadori's DP 214 won a splendid race with Mike Parkes's Ferrari 250 GTO at Monza and the DP 214s were first and second at Montlhery.

During its 4½ year production run the DB4 was much modified, including fairing the headlights on the Vantage, so that its replacement in 1963, the DB5, was almost indistinguishable externally from the final version. With overdrive and the same four-speed David Brown gearbox until a ZF five-speed box was adopted, the 3995 cc engine with three SU carburettors, or three Webers on the Vantage, provided greater flexibility. With other changes in the specification, the difference between the DB5 and DB4 was distinct. The first Volantes, the name attached to all later convertibles, were built on the last few DB5 chassis and were offered at the Motor Show in 1965 alongside the DB6. This had a distinctive body with a flat tail and spoiler on a lengthened wheelbase, and with its Volante version was the first Aston Martin since the war that could properly be called a full four-seater. The DB6 Mark 2, the last model visibly related to the DB4, was built in 1969 and 1970, with power-assisted steering as standard and discreetly flared wheel arches to accommodate wider wheels. The options included fuel injection; optimistically, 325 bhp was claimed for the final Vantage version of Marek's six-cylinder engine

27

with three Weber carburettors, special camshafts and a 9.4 to 1 compression ratio.

For complex marketing reasons the superficially different car revealed in September 1967 was called the DBS not the DB7. The platform chassis had been widened and the wheelbase lengthened to accommodate a V8 engine. The body, designed by William Towns, was 6 inches (150 mm) wider than the DB6, but the roof was about 1 inch (30 mm) lower. Fashionably, it had four headlights but it shared the engine and many other parts with the DB6 Mark 2. Although it was 616 pounds (280 kg) heavier than an early DB4, its top speed, 140 mph (225 km/h), was the same.

This Volante is the open version of the DB6: by 1966 it had become fashionable to describe it as a convertible rather than as a drophead coupé.

Many Aston Martins were assembled at Blenheim Palace, Oxfordshire, in September 1967 to greet the new DBS.

The DBSV8 is readily distinguishable from the DBS by its alloy wheels. This was among those exported to the United States.

EVEN GRANDER TOURING

A V8 engine had been contemplated in 1953 but it was in 1963 that Tadek Marek started work on a design and 5064 cc prototypes were tested in two Lolas that raced in 1967. The DBS with a V8 engine was announced in September 1969 and production of the DBSV8 began six months later. The light-alloy engine, now 5340 cc, had twin overhead-camshaft cylinder heads and was fuel-injected. It delivered about 310 bhp, although at the time the works was content to say that it produced as much power as was needed. The car was about 300 pounds (140 kg) heavier than the DBS, from which it can be distinguished by its light-alloy wheels. Road tests by the motoring press recorded a maximum speed of 160 mph (260 km/h), when it was fitted with a five-speed manual gearbox (automatic transmission was an option).

By far the longest period with one owner, 25 years, ended in January 1972 when Company Developments Limited, a property company, took over. The elimination of two unnecessary headlights from the DBS and DBSV8 vastly

improved the appearance of the Aston Martin Vantage and V8, unveiled in April. The Vantage, the last car with wire wheels and Marek's sturdy six-cylinder engine, was withdrawn in mid 1973 after only seventy had been made. The acute financial problems faced by the company in 1974 culminated in the closure of the factory and the appointment of a receiver at the end of the year. But Aston Martin was not to be added to the list of great but defunct makes. Four enthusiasts, Peter Sprague, George Minden, Alan Curtis and Denis Flather, became the owners by June 1975, at a cost of about £1 million. Between 1980 and 1984 there were three more changes before Victor Gauntlett and Peter Livanos, both enthusiasts in the mould of Lionel Martin and Robert Bamford, became the owners in time to celebrate the emergence of the ten thousandth car since 1915.

The V8 was able to evolve continuously, as a hand-built car can be modified without the costly disruptions this would cause to mass-production lines. By 1988 the V8 had few parts in common with the

A Vantage Volante in 1988. When fuel injection replaced carburettors on the standard engine in 1986, the hump on the bonnet became unnecessary on the V8 saloon and Volante but had to remain on the Vantage versions to clear the carburettors.

A stretched, four-door V8 was introduced as the Aston Martin Lagonda in 1974, but only eight were made. This very different Aston Martin Lagonda was announced in October 1976.

1969 DBSV8. In 1973 the Bosch fuel injection was replaced by four twin-choke Weber carburettors, and fuel injection, also by Weber, returned in 1986. There was a major change to the body and interior trim in 1978. Vantage and Volante versions appeared in 1977 and 1978. The V8 Vantage engine, which had retained its carburettors, had been developed to produce 432 bhp by 1986 when a Vantage Volante was added to the range. In October 1976 the V8 was joined by the Aston Martin Lagonda V8, remarkable for its lines, the speed with which it had been produced and its combination of two names.

The partnership with Zagato was renewed in 1985, 51 Vantage chassis with bodies built in Milan being followed by another limited edition of 25 Zagato Volantes and the purchase of a half share of the Italian company. Work had started on a replacement for the V8 in 1986 and the result, the Virage, was revealed at the Motor Show at Birmingham in October 1988. Volante and Vantage versions were also announced. The chassis and body were completely new and the 5340 cc V8 engine had been developed, with four valves per cylinder, to run only on unleaded petrol without impairing its performance. The Virage is destined to

A Vantage Zagato. All of the limited edition were sold before they were made, between 1986 and 1988.

provide grand touring *par excellence* in the 1990s.

The Aston Martin story (with and without the hyphen, which was dropped in the 1930s) has two strands: the production of cars for the connoisseur, with quality the clear priority, and the recurrence of financial problems. The purchase of 75 per cent of the shares by Ford, announced in September 1987, with the assurance that design policy will remain with Aston Martin Lagonda Limited, promised to strengthen one strand and eliminate the other.

The works has not entered a team car since 1963 as the increasing costs of international racing would have been an unacceptable burden on tight budgets (the V8 engine participated with limited success in Nimrod, EMKA and Cheetah cars between 1982 and 1985). However, racing can still serve the same ends for Aston Martin as it has in the past: a new racer appeared at the end of 1988.

'Bulldog', a design study (or 'concept car' in the current jargon) with a twin-turbo V8 engine amidships and a startling gull-wing body designed by William Towns, revealed in 1980. An intended very limited run was reduced to one in 1979, built to demonstrate the works' engineering skills and to eliminate a lingering public belief that Aston Martin had succumbed in 1975.

FURTHER READING

The books listed below are authoritative sources. To them should be added the publications issued to its members by the Aston Martin Owners Club, including the 300-page *Register*.

Bowler, M. *Aston Martin V8*. Cadogan Publications, 1985.
Gershon, D. *Aston Martin 1963-1972*. Oxford Illustrated Press, 1975.
Hunter, I. *Aston Martin 1914 to 1940, A Pictorial Review*. Transport Bookman Publications, 1976.
Nixon, C. *Racing with the David Brown Aston Martins* (two volumes). Transport Bookman Publications, 1980.
Wyer, J. *The Certain Sound*. Edita, Lausanne, 1981.

PLACES TO VISIT

These museums normally have Aston Martins among the cars displayed. Intending visitors should find out dates and times of opening before making a special journey.

Bentley Motor Museum, The Pump House, Bentley Farm, Halland, Lewes, East Sussex. Telephone: 082584 574.
Donington Collection of Single-Seater Racing Cars, Donington Park, Castle Donington, Derby DE7 2RP. Telephone: 0332 810048.
Doune Motor Museum, Carse of Cambus, Doune, Perthshire. Telephone: 0786 841203.
Midland Motor Museum, Stanmore Hall, Stourbridge Road, Bridgnorth, Shropshire WV15 5JG. Telephone: 0746 761761.
National Motor Museum, John Montagu Building, Beaulieu, Brockenhurst, Hampshire SO4 7ZN. Telephone: 0590 612345.
Totnes Motor Museum, Steamer Quay, Totnes, Devon TQ9 5AL. Telephone: 0803 862777.

Representatives of most of the models can be seen at the Aston Martin Owners Club St John Horsfall Memorial Trophy race meeting at Silverstone, Northamptonshire, in June or July. Telephone the club secretary on 0353 777353 to confirm the date.

The very clean lines of the Virage, shown in a photograph released when it was announced in October 1988.